HOW TO PITCH ANYTHING
Tested method with +1.500 entrepreneurs for Unlocking the Investors Vault

This book is a **practical synthesis** of my experience as a trainer to thousands of entrepreneurs open to a different (and seductive) way of making a pitch. I have summarized in the following chapters the 7 (uncommon) secrets that make a winning pitch. But the best secret I'll tell you now: it's the practice of your own pitch with the direct and personal help of a coach who puts himself in your client's (investor's) hat. This is what I have been doing with thousands of entrepreneurs for many years.

Sergi Sai Mora.

Index

1. Introduction

The Pitch is the art of making a good first impression and seducing in a few seconds. Even if you have 7 minutes to speak, if your pitch does not seduce in the first few seconds, they will hardly pay attention to you.

The pitch is like the cover letter and your resume. If it is written with spelling mistakes, your potential employer will probably discard you and you will have lost the opportunity to work for that company forever. The worst thing, in the case of investors, is that they know each other (because they like to co-invest), and if one of them discards you, sooner or later the others will find out.

And without that injection of capital you are looking for and without the professional accompaniment of an investor, it will probably take you much longer to reach the heights of your entrepreneurial dream. What's worse, millions of people (your potential customers) could be harmed if your business doesn't exist for them.

2. What is and what is not a pitch

The word "pitch" means "speech" in English. In the field of investors, "elevator pitch" is the speech you would give to an investor in an elevator, or rather, in the time it takes for the elevator to go up to the top floor. Therefore, it is the presentation you are going to make to an investor in less than a minute. It is clear that in such a short time an entrepreneur cannot tell an investor everything about his project. You have to select and know how to say it in a way that is understood and arouses interest to learn more. Take note because this is important: the effective pitch tries to create in the investor the desire to know more.

A pitch is not a detailed presentation of your project. In a pitch you don't explain your entire project in a summarized way. You tell just enough so that the investor gets up from his chair, approaches the entrepreneur and says: "What day this week would be good for you to have a coffee with me and tell me more"?

In reality, a pitch is an excuse invented by investors to get to know the entrepreneur (first) and his project (second). Let's remember that an investor invests first in people and then in their ideas or projects. If the impression he has of the entrepreneur is bad, the impression he will have of his project will hardly be good. If the impression he has of the entrepreneur is very good, the impression he will have of the project is unlikely to be bad.

3. Why this book is special

Because I have seen more than 1,500 presentations of entrepreneurs' projects in front of investors in the last 7 years and I have been able to coach hundreds of entrepreneurs in their pitch. I don't know if this experience is enough because I am sure of one thing: there is no single way to seduce an investor. Each investor is different, and what seduces some investors, makes others cringe. But there are 7 uncommon practices that are worth knowing and, in this book, I will try to give you a glimpse of them.

The 1,500 presentations I have seen (and a few more are added each year) were selected from among many others to be presented to investors. And although it is not very nice to say this, 1,200 of those presentations either bored me to tears or were not credible; 280 left a good taste in my mouth, and only 20 managed to keep me with my eyebrows raised, sitting on the edge of my chair and making me want to meet the entrepreneur after his or her presentation.

The entrepreneur who starts his adventure needs to communicate better than anyone else. Knowing how to communicate well is part of "being a leader". You will probably need to seduce future partners (friends, family, acquaintances), employees (who will initially be paid very little), customers (who will be suspicious of new solutions) and potential investors or *Business Angels* (who will have heard thousands of presentations similar to yours).

In these pages we focus on professional investors or *Business Angels and* with a little imagination you can adapt this information to improve your communication with clients, employees, etc.

Business Angels do not so much invest in ideas or products as they invest in the people (teams) who have those ideas or products. A professional investor is looking for teams that can grow their companies quickly. And for that to happen, there are three factors that the investor pays special attention to during a pitch:

1. The team is competent, committed, passionate and determined to achieve its objectives.
2. That the team knows how to sell
3. That the team knows how to measure its progress, adapt continuously and quickly to the market, developing solutions with a clear differential advantage in the eyes of customers (not in the eyes of the entrepreneur).

The investor usually meets an entrepreneur at an investor forum where, in a few hours, he sees about 7-10 different entrepreneurs present their projects for about 10 minutes each. If the investor does not see the three elements mentioned above in the entrepreneur (and his team), and in spite of this decides to meet with the entrepreneur to analyze the project, he will put a thousand obstacles to not invest in the project. That is to say, he will find many excuses about the "risk" of the project, the market, the competition, the prices, etc... when in reality (unconsciously) what he is discarding is the entrepreneurial team.

All 7-10 projects may have the same potential, but not all entrepreneurs will be able to communicate it*. It may even happen that a project with a lower growth potential arouses more interest and desire than a project with a higher potential. The difference lies in how the entrepreneur has staged and presented his project. Thus, the success of a project to be financed depends to a large extent on the non-verbal and verbal communication of the entrepreneur.

---

* Interestingly, according to some studies, most entrepreneurs believe they communicate well, but only a minority of investors think so.

Let's remember that investors invest in people, and if the entrepreneur does not know how to communicate his project well, if this entrepreneur does not have the talent to sell (a critical skill for a start-up company), the perceived "risk" is much higher.

The pitch is the first impression the investor has of the entrepreneur. And if the entrepreneur does not know what impact he/she has when communicating, he/she will probably not have a second chance with the same investor to continue the conversation.

4. The 3 emotions that a winning pitch should arouse

Before preparing the pitch, the entrepreneur must know his audience well, his potential investor in our case.

A professional investor has no trouble making ends meet. What investors want is to put their money into circulation in order to make a profit, contribute a little value to society and have a good time.

Now that we know what the investor is looking for, the pitch must be designed and executed to awaken three sensations in his stomach (something deeper than his intellect since his money, his time and his reputation are at stake):

a) The feeling that you, as an entrepreneur, are a safer bet than other options available to him. That with you he/she will make money and in a faster and safer way than with other options. Therefore, try to minimize any perception of "risk" in your project. The more substantiated your assumptions are, the more credible and less risk he will perceive.

b) The feeling that they will have a good time with you, that you will know how to get along, that you are open to listen to their advice. Therefore, your people skills (as project leader) will be perceived during the pitch. Be a humble leader, prudent, open to people... in short, think about what personal qualities you think your investor would like you to have.

c) The feeling that your project is something unique, differential and that it brings value to a market that the investor probably knows better than the entrepreneur. Therefore, a pitch is also a "sale" of your product or service. The investor must "buy" your solution (as if he were a customer) or must be able to put himself in the shoes of the entrepreneur.

a potential customer and visualize themselves discarding other options and buying, without a doubt, your product or solution.

There are as many types of investors as there are people, and therefore, we might think that we should make a different pitch for each investor. But if we understand how a person's brain works, we will see that there are certain general principles that should be present in every pitch.

The brain has 3 parts, which according to the chronological order of appearance, are:

a) <u>The reptilian brain</u>: the first part developed by the human being, common to all animals. It is the instinct. It is very primitive, in the sense that it knows whether something "is good" or "is bad". It knows no middle ground. Either it is white or it is black. Either something threatens it (and therefore provokes an attack, freeze or flight reaction) or something does not threaten it (and therefore it can relax and trust).

b) <u>The limbic brain</u>: the second part we develop. The limbic brain is more developed in mammals and is capable of feeling pleasure, fear, tranquility, illusion, passion, security, that we are part of a group, etc.

c) <u>The neo-cortex brain:</u> the last to appear and therefore the least developed. Only human beings have it. It allows reasoning, understanding of abstract concepts, numbers, statistics. It is the analytical part of our mind, which always finds a "counter-argument" to any argument.

When the entrepreneur makes a pitch to the investor, it is first filtered by his reptilian (instinctive) brain, then the limbic (emotional) brain, and when it passes both filters, it is analyzed by the neo-cortex (analytical).

Before the entrepreneur opens his mouth, the investor "smells" whether the entrepreneur is trustworthy or not (brain reptilian). It is instinctive (and therefore largely unconscious). When the entrepreneur appears in front of the stage, investors pick up on whether or not that "animal" is a threat to their pocketbook. The investor instinctively knows whether that entrepreneur makes them "hot" or leaves them "cold". Just as if I show them a little piece of crunchy chocolate crisp with pistachio, investors would start salivating ipso facto (it's instinctive), the investor knows if the entrepreneur makes him feel good or bad in just 7 seconds.

Secondly, the pitch that does not emotionally engage the investor is not a good pitch. The pitch that becomes a monologue (where the entrepreneur only talks about himself) is boring. The pitch that does not know how to include the investor in the conversation does not pass the limbic filter. The pitch is a dialogue between the entrepreneur and the investor, only that most of the conversation is carried out by the entrepreneur.
Nor does the pitch pass the emotional filter when the entrepreneur perceives himself as having a greater ambition to make money (or to enlarge his "ego") than his ambition to serve or bring value to others (his client, his team, his partners).

Third, the pitch impacts the investor's rational brain at a conscious level. But the decision has already been made at the unconscious level by the reptilian and limbic brain. That is, before the information reaches the neo-cortex, the investor already knows whether the information is credible or not and whether he likes the entrepreneur or not. The investor makes the decision based on instinct and emotion, and then it is the neo-cortex (analysis) that justifies the decision taken by looking for logical and "sensible" arguments (to explain to itself the logic of the decision already taken).

In short, the entrepreneur will not be able to seduce the investor with data, concepts and logical and cold explanations without first having pacified his or her entrails and warmed his or her heart.

Do you understand now why I was bored or didn't pay attention to 1,200 projects out of the 1,500 I've listened to over the past few years?

They bored me because they only spoke to my neo-cortex and if I stopped paying attention it is because what I was receiving at a more instinctive and emotional level was not coherent with what I understood at a more superficial level from the words those entrepreneurs were pronouncing. The entrepreneur did not know how to win over my gut (instinct) or my heart before winning over my intellect. And the same thing that happened to me, who am human, also happened to most investors. Many seem attentive listening to the pitch but their thoughts are elsewhere. If they applaud at the end of the pitch, it is because they need to cheer themselves up so as not to fall asleep. That is the harsh reality of most pitches. Learn to awaken the 3 sensations that say "he has the risk under control", "he is a good leader" and "he brings a differential value" by involving the investor's emotions, and you will get sincere applause.

5. The worst time to make a pitch

Before making the pitch, the entrepreneur must have something valuable to show. If he makes the pitch in the "much ado about nothing" style, he has burned an opportunity, wasted the investor's time and will carry the stigma of being an inexperienced, foolish, crazy or worse, arrogant entrepreneur.

Therefore, if the pitch fund does not have "substance" it will not seduce any investor. And by "substance" I mean results*. The best pitch is the one that starts by saying: "Gentlemen, in recent months we have found that it costs us €1 to get a customer and that with that customer we get €2 on average, and there is also a significant viral effect that makes us reduce the cost of acquisition".

If you have extraordinary metrics (figures or results), you don't need a coach to refine your pitch. Your results are your collateral.

If your metrics are still poor, you need to have a very good pitch to seduce the investor. But make no mistake, you will find far fewer investors willing to risk their money because they will consider that there is still too much risk in your project.

If your metrics are non-existent, it is not the best time to make a pitch, unless you have founding partners or prestigious investors within your company (such as founding partners of well-known companies like "Privalia" or "Offerum", or investors like the "Inveready" group or "Caixa Capital Risc").

---

*There are exceptions. I have seen investors who are "fooled" by a good pitch. Either their intuition fails them, or they are not connected to their emotions or instinct, or they are not risk averse at all and therefore play the lottery.

6. What makes a pitch disastrous

I have detected 3 factors that make people stop paying attention to a pitch (no matter how good the entrepreneur's project may be).

The first factor is that they do not convey any clear idea. They say a lot of things but not in an orderly fashion and there is no one thing that stands out above the others. Yes, it is more or less clear what the project is about, but it is not clear what makes it "special". To me (or to the investor), it is a project of which we will remember vague ideas (but in the end we have categorized it as "this project is NOT interesting").

The second factor is that they don't make me feel part of the project. They don't make me feel anything. It's like watching a movie where nothing happens, no action, no suspense, no drama, no laughter, nothing. My limbic brain is asleep. The investor has not visualized himself having fun with the entrepreneur. The entrepreneur has not been able to awaken the desire to "want to know more" in the investor.

The third factor is that I see an entrepreneur desperate to find an investor, as if getting the investor's money were the entrepreneur's ultimate goal. In the animal world, you know how a female reacts when approached by a desperate male...well, the same thing happens with investors and it is that part of our nature, whether we are men or women, is animal and we do not like to feel hunted (and we do like to feel seduced).

7. The 7 secrets for a winning pitch

If a perfect pitch were a delicious cake, the secrets to the cake's success would be:

a) In the quality of its ingredients
b) On the mood of the cook at the time of making the cake.
c) On the cook's ability to follow the recipe exactly
d) In the presentation of the cake
e) The amount of cake eaten by the diner
f) On what happens around the diner as he eats the cake
g) What the diner thinks about while tasting the cake

Let's look at how each of these components should be present in the winning pitch.

a. First secret: *keywords*

Just as part of the success of a delicious cake is in the quality of its ingredients, a pitch with quality keywords is a winning pitch.

The main ingredient of a pitch is the results achieved by the team presenting the project. I call them "keywords", and the most important Keyword is *traction*, which is the rapid progression in your main metrics (and the one that stands out above all are sales, number of clients and how much it costs you to get a client). The investor wants to see that you have taken off, that your business is picking up speed. And if you don't have sales, you won't be liked in the same way. The investor will want you to explain other kinds of results you have achieved. Ask yourself: what are your achievements, your successes, your "medals" to date? And be as concrete (not abstract) and synthetic as possible in your answer.

Examples of *Keywords*:

Example of sales traction (the main Keyword): We have 100 customers, with average sales of 3.000€/customer and every week we have 15% more customers with a customer acquisition cost that has gone from 300€ to 100€.

Examples of **other types of keywords**:
- We have 300 customers in 3 different countries
- One of our clients is "Nestlé", leader in the chocolate sector in Spain.
- Of our 5 clients, 4 have come from referrals.
- Our customers pay 30% more for our service than they were paying with our competitor.
- We have achieved 40,000 downloads of our application in 2 months.

- We are three people dedicated full time to this project and have been working together for 10 years.
- I left a position as a director of a listed company and now I have been paid absolutely nothing for a whole year and I have contributed 300,000 euros.
- One of our partners won the equivalent of the "Oscars" but in the genetics sector.
- We have 3 worldwide patents for our product and have signed a distribution agreement with Samsung.
- We have appeared on TV3, La Vanguardia and in 20 other media in the last 4 months, which has brought us 1.000.000 visits which has translated into 30.000€ in sales.

If you only have 30 seconds to make your pitch, I recommend that you simply use your keywords. Say the best thing you have achieved so far. You don't need to explain what you do (or what your company does). It is about creating desire in the first few seconds so that the investor will want to listen until the end. If you start "strong" (with "powerful" keywords), you will make the investor interested in paying attention to the rest of your pitch.

I remember an entrepreneur who started his pitch saying: "Good morning, my name is Javi and among our partners are the founders of Privalia...". From that moment on, the audience paid attention to everything that entrepreneur said. With such a "powerful" start, you don't need a spectacular pitch to get the investor to come to you afterwards and say: "When can we meet?"

Therefore, build your winning pitch by first detecting the quality of raw material you have available. Make a list of your keywords and rank them from the most to the least important (to the investor's ears).

b. Second secret: the type of energy behind the words

Just as a cake is better if its cook is in a good mood (or cooks with love), the pitch must be transmitted with strength, with passion.

The strength of the pitch is not in what the entrepreneur says but in how he makes the investor feel when he says it. And what the investor is looking for is to feel enthusiastic about the project. And for that to happen, the entrepreneur must first <u>feel</u> enthusiastic about what he is saying and must have the <u>intention </u>of transmitting that energy of passion to the investor.

Enthusiasm is contagious. If the entrepreneur does not feel that passion when he thinks or talks about his project, it will hardly be felt by the investor.

If the entrepreneur delivers his pitch feeling fearful and insecure, this is what he will transmit to the investor. On the one hand, clear, well-structured ideas that promise great expectations of future profits will come out of his mouth. But on the other hand, what the investor receives is insecurity and fear. That is to say, there is an inconsistency between what is said and what is not said (but felt or perceived unconsciously). And that incoherence leaves your pitch on the floor in a few seconds.

Therefore, whoever makes the pitch must feel passion and determination to take the project forward (no matter what happens, with or without an investor). If you don't feel it while speaking, there is no strength. If you speak from that conviction, the pitch has strength and can move the investor to take a risk*.

Let's remember that the pitch is aimed primarily at the limbic (emotional) brain of the investor. That is achieved when the entrepreneur speaks from his or her

---

* In the workshops I teach I teach how to speak with strength and conviction, which is to connect with your heart while speaking. I also teach how not to be afraid or insecure speaking in public, how to connect with the investor and attract their attention, how to make the investor - all of them - feel that you are speaking to them.

heart, not from your intellect. Speaking from the heart is very simple but it is not easy for everyone, especially for entrepreneurs with a very technical, analytical or scientific profile.

The secret is for the entrepreneur to feel passion, love, gratitude (or any other positive quality) especially during the first few seconds when he is presenting his project and, above all, it is very important that he has the intention of transferring that positive state to his audience. If he starts talking feeling that passion, or love, or gratitude, and his intention is to share that positive feeling with the listener, he will be transmitting that energy to the investor's unconscious.

Since the first impact that the investor will receive from the entrepreneur will be positive (albeit unconscious), the investor, without knowing very well why, will begin to see the entrepreneur with "good eyes". Or in other words, everything the entrepreneur says will be taken on the "good side", or he will rationalize more positively everything he says.

When I conduct a workshop with entrepreneurs to teach them all this, the first thing I do (as a teacher) is to fill my heart with a good feeling and (inwardly) wish that each student takes away, at the very least, that state I feel. I know that starting my workshops this way predisposes the students favorably towards me. Now you as an entrepreneur can use this secret to win the heart of the investor in the first seconds.

c. Third secret: the magic structure

Just as to make a delicious cake you need to follow a recipe very well (and not skip steps), to make a winning pitch you need to follow a very concrete structure that will make everything you say understood.

Order matters and much more than most people think. The most common mistake made by entrepreneurs is to present their solution without first presenting the problem they are solving. Any company is born because it has seen that there is a customer who has a problem*.

The entrepreneur's raison d'être is his customer, and more specifically, his customer's problem. The entrepreneur must know how to talk about his customer's problem better than the customer himself. If he is able to talk in more detail about the problem, the entrepreneur is automatically seen as an "expert" in the eyes of the customer.

Most of the pitches I have seen either omit the problem, or talk about it in detail. On the other hand, it is also important to identify the "pain" in that unresolved problem. The more painful the problem, the more urgent the need for a solution. Therefore, you have to get the investor to feel that pain in their skin, right then and there.

But after talking about the problem (and making the pain felt), it is not yet the right time to introduce the solution. That would be another common mistake. Now is the right time to talk about what existing solutions are available to the customer. It is time to talk about which ways, both "craft" and "around the house", such as

---

*There are companies that will say that their product does not satisfy any problem but responds to a market opportunity. In that case, if there is no clear and commonly recognized and accepted problem, it is not such an attractive project for the investor. There are exceptions (for example, buying apartments as a form of speculation during the real estate bubble).

The investor wants to see that you are a "professional", you know the customer currently to solve his problem. The investor wants to see that you know well the market where you compete. You must know how to recognize (without criticizing) what your competitors do well*. If the entrepreneur is able to speak well of his competitors, he will gain credibility when he speaks of his own solution.

When you talk about your solution (which is the third point of a winning pitch; and, I repeat, it is not the second, not the first, but the third point of a pitch), you must identify your differential advantage. You have an advantage on one point (and not on two or three - the investor will not believe in a "Superman" project). You must identify what you do better (or want to do better) than anyone else to solve the client's problema**. And you must know how to explain it in a way that makes it understandable and memorable. This brings us to the fourth secret of a good pitch. But first I want to stress the importance of the magic structure:

1. Who is the client and what is the problem (in detail).
2. How the customer currently solves their problem (existing solutions).
3. How the company solves their problem better than existing solutions and what will make the customer make the effort to switch suppliers (and choose you)[10].

If you skip this order your pitch will not have the same strength. This scheme follows a logical and overwhelming order. And I know from experience that even if I repeat this point 10 times in my workshops, many entrepreneurs will prefer to try other formulas that in my opinion are less effective and that is a pity.

---

* You must give the facts and let the investor form for himself the idea that the existing solutions are not sufficient to solve the customer's problem.

** Of course, it must be "differential" in the eyes of the customer (who must be willing to stop buying from the competition to buy from the entrepreneur). If there is no such behavioral change, it is not a differential advantage.

[10] For the rest of the possible points to be discussed, I leave the order to your discretion. The 4th point could be "how do you get 1 customer" (marketing, distribution). The 5th point could be "your business model" (marketing, distribution). revenue). The 6th could be "your sales forecasts". The 7th "how much money you will need to reach your objectives". The 8th "who you are in the team (and why you are the right team)"....

d. The fourth secret: the metaphor

Just as presentation can either ruin a cake or make it very desirable, as when we were children and were dazzled by the candles on our birthday cake, a winning pitch needs a good presentation.

Supposing you are a girl and your boyfriend asks you to marry him and offers you a flattened and cracked cardboard box (where a ring is supposed to be inside), what would you think of the jewel inside? Surely, it's a trinket.

The "container" counts for a lot. It is what makes the "content" understandable, accepted and remembered.
The metaphor is the "little box with the ring", it is the first thing the girl sees. The metaphor is the "little box" of the pitch and provides a context or special meaning to everything the entrepreneur will say next. The entrepreneur should know how to explain what he/she does (or what makes him/her special and unique) in the form of a metaphor.

An entrepreneur I know well, Roger, came to see me one day and told me he had set up a business. I asked him: "And what do you do, Roger"? And he replied: "I've set up DIR* ballroom dancing". His metaphor not only helped me understand in an instant what he does, but by making me imagine what he does, it stuck with me forever.

It is not what you say, but how you get me to imagine it, that makes a message remembered**. By using a metaphor, the entrepreneur is using the power of the image. If an image has the power to communicate 1,000 words, a metaphor has the power to communicate 1,000 images. That is to say, if the entrepreneur develops a

---

*Chain of gyms very widespread in Catalonia (Spain)
** According to psychologist Albert Mehrabian, the *how* is 11 times more impactful than the *what.*
http://en.wikipedia.org/wiki/Albert_Mehrabian

metaphor to explain your differential advantage, will make the investor picture your differential advantage in his mind*. You have not used any external image (which is already powerful) but an internal image (the one I have imagined), and according to Einstein, "imagination is more important than knowledge".

I recommend that if you want to make your pitch understandable and memorable, look for a metaphor to describe what you do. Ask your mother, your grandmother, your daughter or someone who doesn't know very well what you do and ask them: "What I just explained to you, for you, is it like what?" and you will see how they explain what you do in a metaphorical and simple way.

Once you have identified the ideal metaphor, you should structure your pitch around it. Try to start and end with the metaphor. And during the rest of the pitch, invite the investor to discover a little more about your project by navigating that metaphor. In this way you will place or present your project in a unique and special light. A winning pitch can even revolve around that metaphor and develop into a story (but I don't want to go into that much depth here).

In short, it is important to remember that to have a winning pitch you must get your investor to "see" very clearly what the opportunity is, and try to make them imagine themselves and feel part of your business venture. Metaphor is the best way to achieve all that and make him remember you.

---

*The entrepreneur should use this metaphor and look for similar expressions, and repeat it 2 or 3 times so that the message is engraved forever in the investor's brain.

e. The fifth secret: less is more

Even the best cake in the world, if you eat too much of it, is no longer delicious. So the entrepreneur should not pour an excess of information in his pitch. And the information that he or she does pour out should always be concrete and not abstract.

A pitch should not be a tight summary of the *Business Plan*. You must know how to discard that information that does not seduce. Let's suppose you have 10 things to tell about your project, where 6 are of high quality* and 4 of low quality. If you tell everything, the quality perceived by the investor is "medium" (neither high nor low). If instead of counting all 10 things, you count only the 6 of high quality, the average perception of the entrepreneur is "high".

When you speak, you must do so in a concrete and tangible way. Everything that is tangible ("it can be touching or seeing") and concrete (for example: say "Nestlé" instead of "a customer") is much more seductive than that which is conceptual and abstract**.

I suggest you take a post-it note and write down all the main messages you think the investor would like to hear. Each message should be able to be written in 10 words or less. And then rank them in order of importance. Try to see how they relate to your metaphor and finally select which ones you will say and which ones you choose to keep quiet. And see how you can make each message more tangible and concrete.

For example, let's suppose that the message you want to convey is: "Our software allows quick decision making for airline pilots". To make this message more tangible, you could use two images, one showing 300 knobs with signals and indicators of different colors, and the other showing a screenshot of the software screen showing a simple knob with a "red or green" color depending on the

---

* Think about what "high quality" might be in the eyes of the investor....

** The abstract activates the "neo-cortex". The tangible activates the "limbic" (emotional) brain.

decision to be made. The fact of showing the screenshot of the software makes what is expressed by voice more tangible and concrete.

If you use PowerPoint (I do not recommend Prezi), each slide should have only 1 message (not two). Remember that the PowerPoint is there to complement and reinforce what you say, not to replace you. The investor should <u>not be</u> able to understand your project just by reading the presentation. If they can, you are not using it correctly to accompany a pitch. It is one thing to use this tool to reinforce your pitch and quite another to use a PowerPoint loaded with information that you could send by mail to the investor so that he can read it at home (called "pitch deck").

In short, you must know how to select only those ideas that are of high quality (and discard the rest - I know it is not easy as we seem to leave out "important" things). If you want your ideas to be understandable, they must be presented visually and metaphorically, concretely and tangibly (not abstractly), with simple language (not theoretical, technical or complex). All this makes an emotional impact. And if the entrepreneur has a finished product (such as a website), it is better to show that product than to talk about it. If you show it or make a demo (essential according to investor Guy Kawasaki) you are being very concrete and the investor does not have to think in abstract concepts*.

Therefore, to have a winning pitch you must resist the temptation to talk more than necessary, and speak simply and concretely, so that anyone can understand you**.

---

* The neo-cortex is the one that processes abstract concepts, and this requires a lot of energy. When the entrepreneur speaks only to the investor's neo-cortex, the investor is mentally exhausted and prefers to disconnect (or play with the cell phone).
** I suggest you make the pitch to your grandmother or your young son. If they understand the same thing, it's understood.

f. Sixth secret: godparents

A cake is tastier if other people have tasted it before and recommend it to you.

You must be able to create that perception of value or what I call a "social context of scarcity and exclusivity". When something is desirable for a select social environment, it is more desirable for the rest. And if it is also "scarce" (there is not enough for everyone), it is even more desirable and people are willing to pay a premium.

The "shortage" is generated for example when you say "we are looking for €500,000 of which we currently have €400,000 committed and we are now in the phase of raising the remaining €100,000, which we hope to close in the next two weeks". Or when you say something like "actually the money we are asking for is secondary, because with the current partners we could cope with this growth phase; but we are open to a contribution of €100,000 from an investor who can help us open the doors we have mentioned".

The entrepreneur must know how to convey the confidence that "if this is not where he/she will find investment, it's okay because he/she is already in good company". A winning pitch is one that is NOT in a hurry to find an investor. The entrepreneur must know how to convey the feeling that the project is a unique opportunity difficult to repeat. Even the project will continue to succeed with or without an investor. With the investor the project will go faster, nothing more. For this to be credible, what I call important "godfathers" are needed.

A sponsor is a company of recognized prestige that bets on you. For example: "Telefónica is betting on us because we have been selected as exclusive *partners worldwide for* the development of all applications containing artificial intelligence". This technological sponsor augurs enormous potential for your company. With such a sponsor you become one of those "trains that rarely pass in front of the investor".

In the end, having "Telefónica" as a sponsor is a "keyword". But the emphasis at this point is on the feeling of "scarcity and exclusivity", that the project "has many brides to choose from", or that the entrepreneurs are the ones who have "the paella by the handle" and that "they are not beggars after the investor's money".

The secret is to get important sponsors, companies and also prestigious people who surround the project (either as partners The company's sponsors may be technological partners, suppliers or an "*advisory board*"). Very often, one of these sponsors is a first investor, someone who decided to bet and is now willing to continue investing and to show his or her face in public in front of potential new investors.

The network of relationships that the company has woven is worth gold, and should be brought out during the pitch. This creates the idea in the investor that "if they have bet and are still betting, why shouldn't I bet too?

Therefore, to have a winning pitch, before going to convince an investor you must convince a few sponsors. An entrepreneur's first sale is to his team. The second sale is to his customer. The third sale is to sponsors. And the fourth is to investors. Whoever goes looking for an investor without having clients and without having a good team, wastes his time going after investors. If you have a team, customers and a sponsor, you will be approached by investors like bees to honey.

g. Seventh secret: anticipation

Just as a cake tastes bad if the diner entertains negative thoughts while eating it, a pitch is not a winner if it raises a doubt or objection in the investor's mind and this doubt is left floating unresolved.

Everything you say can raise a counter-argument, a doubt or an objection (especially if your pitch is directed to the neo-cortex and not to the limbic brain). It is important that you try to guess what are the potential objections that each sentence of your pitch may raise. The way to guess is to make your pitch in front of friends, acquaintances, associates, relatives and ask them "What doubts or objections do you have about what I have just said?

Or you yourself, entrepreneur, can play "the chair game" (sometimes used in coaching practice), which consists of the following:

- You place two chairs, one in front of the other. In one chair you sit and in the other chair (in front of you) you imagine that the investor is sitting.
- Pitch to your invisible investor.
- After saying each sentence (out loud), sit in the investor's chair with the intention of listening to what you have just said, feel yourself in the investor's place, in his or her own skin. At this point, the investor (actually you occupying the investor's chair) should express any doubts or objections he/she has (and write them down in a notebook).
- At the end of the exercise you will have a notebook with ten or more potential objections.

Once you know the potential objections that an investor may have, you should be able to introduce in your pitch a response to those objections. So, for example, if one of the objections is "you have not mentioned Google as a competitor of your product", in your improved pitch you should say something like: "probably, investors, you will wonder why I do not mention Google as a competitor of your product", in your improved pitch you should say something like: "probably, investors, you will wonder why I do not mention Google as a competitor of your product".

potential competitor. The reason is very simple...".
Finish the sentence by resolving that objection. By
doing so, the investor will feel as if you are reading
his thoughts. If you don't do it this way, as soon as
the investor has 3 unresolved doubts or objections,
he will disconnect from your pitch.

Therefore, to have a winning pitch you must
anticipate possible objections and resolve them in
your pitch.

8. Formula to start with a winning pitch

The first few seconds of your pitch are crucial. During those first few seconds the investor is relatively open to you. He is eager to be surprised. He is waiting to find in you the "winner", the person in whom he will invest his time, his trust and his money. In other words: during the first few seconds the investor keeps the door to his heart ajar and waits for you to open it and come in.

If you fail to seduce the investor during the first few seconds, his door will close and it will be much more difficult for you to get inside his heart and seduce him. In fact, if you start off badly, the investor is likely to build a "fortress" around himself and everything you say (no matter how good it is) will hit the wall he has erected and nothing you say will have any impact on him.

And now the formula for starting a winning pitch. First the design phase and then the execution phase.

1. Design:
a. Define your magic structure (who your customer is and what problem they have, how they currently solve their problem, and why they would prefer to change and come to you).
b. Then define in 1 or 2 things what you think your investor does not know about your client. Remember that, as your client's expert, you must be able to verbalize his problems in more detail than the client himself would be able to do.
c. Next define 1 or 2 things you think your investor doesn't know about your customer's experience with current or existing solutions (your competition).
d. Define your metaphor and describe what your customer would see, hear, or feel in the following way

different if he would use your solution (your product or service).

e. Finally, define your keywords and fill your heart with passion.

2. <u>Execution (with an invented example):</u>

The execution starts with three "Did you know what...? and one "Can you imagine what...? It will be clearer at the end, but first I want to detail the design phase:

a. <u>Target customer</u>: urbanites between 30 and 50 years old who like to socialize and keep fit.
<u>Problem</u>: they have no time for themselves, they work outside the home all day and have a family to take care of.
<u>Existing solutions</u>: go to the gym or go to the disco. The former ends up being boring and with the latter the person feels out of place.
<u>Our solution</u>: an outdoor gym where you can meet people like you and keep fit in a fun way.

b. People who keep fit live an average of 10 years longer. And people who play sports outdoors live 7 years longer on average than those who play sports in a gym.

c. The average length of stay of a person in a gym is 5 months. The average age of people in a discotheque is 20 years.

d. We are the outdoor gym*.

---

* Image obtained from <u>Gonnafit</u> (the outdoor gym). The rest of the pitch I use as an example was invented by me and does not necessarily match the real Gonnafit company pitch.

<u>The execution* is:</u>

Did you know that people who play sports live an average of 10 years longer?
Did you know that people who play sports outdoors live 7 years longer on average than those who play sports indoors?
And did you know that the average length of stay of a client in a gym is 5 months and that for a 40 year old person going to a discotheque is like selling umbrellas in a desert?
Can you imagine being able to take care of your health and outdoors in your city while socializing, feeling integrated and having a better time than partying or going to the gym?

You don't have to imagine it because this is what we have created. We are the outdoor group gym (*metaphor*). We are two entrepreneurs, winners of world triathlons; we are present in 30 cities in 5 different countries; with more than 10,000 clients with an average permanence period of more than 3 years (*keywords*).

Remember to say the first words **with passion** and with the intention of transmitting that energy to the investor.

If you follow this outline (and you have a good metaphor, good keywords and passion), you will raise the investor's eyebrows, make him or her lean forward slightly and pay attention for the rest of your pitch.

---

* **In bold** the essential elements to start a winning pitch.

9. Formula for seducing an investor face-to-face in 3 minutes

I recently coached 18 startups to improve their pitch for an event (the 4YFN) where they had 3 minutes to meet face-to-face with different investors.

Most entrepreneurs think that they have 3 minutes to seduce the investor and that in order to do so, they should try to make a good "monologue". However, my advice is to forget about wanting to "seduce" as this adds (unnecessary) pressure on the entrepreneur and try instead to establish a "dialogue" in which the important thing is to find out whether the investor is interested (or not) in continuing the conversation afterwards. In other words, instead of wanting to "seduce" we try to "find out if there is interest" and instead of a monologue, we establish a dialogue. In this way we reduce the pressure and make the investor feel less pressured as well.

How do you start this dialogue and what is the structure that can facilitate your pitch? Here is the formula:

1. Connect with the Metaphor +
2. Keywords + 3. Find out + 4. Demo

Connect: When you approach the investor, you shake their hand (with the intention of transferring your warm affection through it) while looking them in the eye and saying something like "Hi, my name is [NAME] and we want to be the future [METAPHOR]". For example: "Hello, my name is Sergi Mora and we want to be the future "DIR of ballroom dancing".

Keywords: You smile and share your 3-4 most powerful keywords, i.e. those short phrases that are achievements and bring credibility to your project. Finally, mention how much money you are looking for and for what purpose. For example:

"We were born 1 year ago and we have become the first Spanish chain of dance halls, with more than 3,000 students who pay an average of 30€/month. The cost of acquiring a customer is €20 and the value of a customer ("life time value") is €270. We are a team of 10 people and we are looking for €1,000,000 - of which we have already raised €600,000 - to become the first company in the sector in Europe".

<u>Find out</u>: Once you have named your keywords, notice the look on the investor's face. If his eyes or face shine, it means that he likes you. If he backs away or shows doubts or little interest...make a mental note that you are very interested in what comes next. Now is the time to find out what your investor is looking for. It is not the time to go on explaining more about your project but to let the investor speak. To do this you should ask: *"Before I explain a little more about what makes us different and how we intend to be leaders in Europe, can I ask you a couple of questions to understand what you are looking for in a project like ours?*
That is, what are those 2-3 factors that you would need to see in our project to make it investable?" And wait for their response. Notice that you are asking for permission to know what is really important. It is important that you listen and take notes because the investor is going to tell you what he wants to hear or see.

<u>Demo:</u> Now is when the pitch becomes a dialogue as you must convey to the investor the feeling that you have listened well and resolved their doubts. If possible, give them a demo of your product and tell them a little more about who you are trying to sell it to (your ideal client); what problem they have (or what they want); what alternative solutions they are currently using (your competitors) and what will make them look at your solution (your differential value).

At the end of the demo you will surely know if the investor liked you or not. And you will know it by his facial expression, by his tone of voice and because he will have expressed it to you (he will say something like "I find it very interesting, here is my card and let's see if we can meet next week to continue talking"). If he doesn't show you this obvious interest, it is a sign that he is NOT interested at this moment. And your mission, in these cases, is to learn in order to improve your next pitch to other investors. That is, I suggest you try to find out why he is not interested. And the way to ask for feedback is the following: "I have the feeling that either I have not been able to convey the potential of our project or it does not fit right now with your investment plans. If you could give me some feedback I'd appreciate it." And listen. Or ask "I have the feeling that our project does not fit 100% with what you are looking for right now. From 0 to 10, how interesting is it to you? A 3? A 4? Or maybe a 5? Wait for the answer and keep asking until you are very clear about what your investor is looking for. If, for example, he says "We'd like to see a little more run", ask: "What do you mean by more run? Or if he says "From 0 to 10 I liked a 7". Then continue to probe with questions like "What would make your interest an 8?". It's all about you coming away from the mini-meeting with as much learning as possible about how you can improve your project (or your pitch). And if you see that the investor is not clear when it comes to giving you feedback either (and your questions have been crystal clear) then you must accept that this investor is really NOT interested and you are probably not interested in going after him/her either. When you finish the meeting, thank him/her for the feedback and ask if he/she would like you to send him/her some more information or keep him/her informed of your progress.

- **How do I know if I am ready to present to an investor?**
  - If you're wondering, it's a sign that you're not ready; it's a sign that you don't really know what the investor is looking for. It's as if you were to ask me: Should I marry this person? If you're asking, you shouldn't marry. My advice is to go to 5 or 6 investor forums as an observer (as an audience) and see what the projects they present have. The day will come (or not) when you will know that you are ready; but, if you doubt, you will also make the investor doubt that you are really ready to be invested.

- **How can I give so much information in just 5 minutes?**
  - In reality, you only have a few seconds to really seduce the investor. Start with your best *keywords*. If they are understood and make them salivate (that "I want to know more" feeling) then, in that case alone, you will have the full 5 minutes of attention. Think that the investor will probably have in his hands about 300 projects per year, and his resources are also limited. He goes to the forums in order to discard between 295 and 299 projects, and if he perceives the slightest risk, he will discard you.

    When you speak, ask yourself: "And what's in it for the investor?" He is looking for results ("*show me the money*"), remember that. So instead of saying "We have gone to 3 international fairs" you have to expose:

"We have been to three trade fairs
and have reached agreements with
two German and one English
distributor that will bring us an
expected €1M in sales over the next
12 months."

- **Should I talk numbers or leave it for the details after the pitch?**
    - If you have a minute, it might be enough to mention the current sales figure, the investment you have made as partners and the investment you need now. If you have more time, it is important that you also spend a few seconds explaining how much money it costs you to get a customer (and how many sales that translates into), what sales forecast you have and what you will do to achieve it, and what you will use the investor's money for. You must make the investor understand that you handle economic figures (at a micro-economic level per unit sold), forecasts and their assumptions. You should even be able to talk about "plan B" or contingency in case the forecasts are not met.
    Numbers are important but try to get your pitch to the investor's heart (emotion) first before you speak to their head with numbers. Make them see that there is a real need for your product or service. First is the emotional sale to the investor as if he were a potential client and then you can make the more cold and calculating sale as an investor himself; that is to say, as a person who will risk part of his patrimony.

- **I have been to three investor forums and in all three I have been prepared very differently. Or, some investors tell me**

one thing and others recommend the opposite.

- o What is probably happening is that you are not prepared to present in front of an investor. If if you have powerful keywords (and the evolution of your sales figures is the most important of all), all the contributions that these investors give you are more coherent or provide you with more value. If your *keywords* are scarce (and therefore, so will be the investor's interest), then their contributions leave you with a feeling of "incoherence" on their part, but in reality, what they are telling you is: "you are discarded", don't waste my time. And that's why you get that feeling of "dizziness" or not really knowing where the problem lies. Investors do not tell you the raw truth of what they think of your project to your face (usually out of "education") but will give you a thousand and one excuses not to invest. And in the end, it usually happens that they have not seen enough *keywords* (or results or "track-record").

- **I think I am ready to receive an investor and I already have some important results, but I don't understand why I need an investor.**
  - o If you are so prepared, you may not need it. Ask yourself what is the next level of your company and if you can achieve it with your current resources. The investor can help you in that qualitative leap (and not only quantitative by injecting capital). The investor invests when you have already passed the "desert" phase (when you have minimized the risk) and now you are left with more uncertainties.

than before, but they are no longer uncertainties about your product, your technology or your business model. They are uncertainties such as: "International expansion policy", "How to incorporate and retain talent", "How to improve processes", "What kind of alliances are best for us", etc. If these are the conversations you have with your partners, an investor will surely like to participate.

- **Investors are "sharks" and want to take advantage of the entrepreneur.**
    - They are people and there are all kinds. Depending on how you are (inwardly) you will see some traits or others in others. If you look for the good of your client (and of society) above your own comfort, you will find less shark-like investors than if you only pursue the investor as an end for your personal enrichment. This is how the law of affinities works: we see outside aspects of ourselves and criticize those we don't recognize or accept in ourselves. So everything you criticize outside should serve as food for thought. Change yourself and you will see that there are investors who are true angels.

- **How much do I ask from an investor?**
    - If you don't know, no one else will. And don't wait for the investor to tell you. He wants to hear your plan (and your plan must have a financial need associated with it). If you don't know whether it's €100,000 or €200,000, you don't have a well-defined plan. Do your homework before presenting in front of an investor.

- **How do I value my company?**
    - o There are several methods that can give you an orientation or range of value of your company, but the market is the one that rules. Investors will tell you what percentage they want for their €200,000. Take care to attract the interest of different investors, and let them all know that "you have a lot of girlfriends or boyfriends." The price/share you agree on is a matter of negotiation.

- **And how long can it take me to get an investor?**
    - o Between tomorrow and never. The average is 6 months. Those that go faster, 2-3 months. The slowest, 12-24 months. After these 24 months, if you have not found the investor, you are "out of the market". If you have visited all the investor forums and they have all said "no", your project (or you) will have to change a lot to convince them again. And if you can't or don't know how to change, learn where you went wrong and *move on*. As Edison said "you haven't failed, you've just found a thousand ways that didn't work." Take away the experience and a round of applause for trying.

    - **I can find no interest from any investor, so what now?**
    - o The world does not end here. In fact, very few of the fastest growing companies in the world (according to *Forbes magazine*) have an investor inside. Most have grown on their own, with the resources of their founders (family, friends or acquaintances), loans and by their own sales to their customers. Just because you're not investable doesn't mean you can't grow, so take heart!

11.   **How to make a pitch to a client in less than 1 minute**

The structure:

You: introduce yourself and ask the other person if they
know anyone who has [THE PROBLEM YOU SOLVE].
Client: answer [remember it is a dialogue] and you get the
[NAME] of that person.
You: Provide some INSIGHT about THE PROBLEM that the
other person probably doesn't know. Take a [PAUSE] to
give him/her time to integrate what you have just
revealed.
Continue by imagining [WHAT the experience would be like
for NAME with your solution] and [WHAT metrics or
milestones you have already achieved] and end with
[WHAT you are looking for].

**Example: imagine you are at a trade show (4YFN) and
you are approached by a potential customer:**

Customer: What do you do?
You: My name is Tomás Lóbez, I am the CEO of Nixi for
Children, and we are dedicated to reducing the anxiety of
children entering an operating room through virtual reality.
Have you met any child who has had to undergo surgery?
Customer: Yes....
You: What is the name of that child? to put a more real
context... [pause]... [pause].
Client: Zac
You: Did you know that most children like Zac, when they go
to an operating room for the first time, have a hard time?
Imagine being separated from their parents, entering
alone in a cold room, with machines, unknown people
dressed in green, some with their mouths covered? it's
scary if it's the first time and you are 6 years old, don't
you think? [pause]
Customer: buff....
You: Yes, but now with us, kids like Zac can have a better
experience. We give them a kit containing virtual reality
goggles where, at home, they can see what the operating
room will be like inside, with the doctors dressed in green,
etc. By experiencing the "virtual operating room" at home,
it prepares you psychologically for the operation. Our
brain does not distinguish between "virtual" and "real" so
when Zac goes to the operating room, it will be familiar
and therefore he will have less anxiety.
We are currently working for the Germans Trias i Pujol
hospital, and we already have 80 children who have tried
it and have rated their experience with us with an average
score of 9.8. And we are here at 4YFN open to find
partners to commercialize our solution in hospitals. What
do you think?

12.   Conclusions

When a guy tries to seduce a girl for a first date, he does not tell her his whole life in a few minutes, nor does he try to show his desire to get her phone number, nor does he talk about theories or abstract things. In the same way, the entrepreneur trying to seduce the investor should not condense in a few minutes his whole business plan, nor be desperate to get financing, nor speak only to his rational part or neo-cortex.

The pitch is the art of showing oneself, sharing one's passion and determination for a project, while engaging the investor and his emotions in that conversation, telling just enough so that the investor raises his eyebrows, his face lights up, his body leans forward, and he gets up from his chair when the pitch is over and asks the entrepreneur, "What day this week would you like to have coffee?"

Practice your pitch 100 times if necessary, and if you have the opportunity, ask a coach to help you polish the content, form and execution.

And remember, your pitch is just an excuse for the investor to get to know you. Be yourself and enjoy the moment. If you are focused on yourself, you will be nervous. If you are focused on your audience and sharing the best of your heart with them, you will enjoy it much more and they will thank you twice as much.

Sergi Sai Mora

coach@sergimora.com

PS. Remember this quote from Albert Einstein: "Do not want to become a man of success but a man of value". Don't measure your success by the money you make but by the value you bring to others.

And by the same author...